A DARK WIN...

by Claire Llewellyn

Contents

CAMBRIDGE UNIVERSITY PRESS

UCL Institute of Education

Winter in the Arctic

Some places on earth are very dark and very cold during the winter. In the **Arctic Circle**, the sun is always low in the sky. During the autumn, the sun sinks lower and lower. By November, it cannot be seen above the **horizon**.

In the winter, the sun does not rise, but some light can still be seen.

DID YOU KNOW?

Each day in December has just a few hours of **twilight**. Then night falls again.

In autumn, the sun is very low in the sky.

NORWAY

Arctic Circle

Karasjok

Arctic Circle

NORWAY

Oslo

Equator

Karasjok is 1800 kilometres north of Oslo.
Oslo is Norway's capital city.

4

Welcome to Karasjok!*

Karasjok is a village in the far north of Norway.

It is in the Arctic Circle.

The winters are very cold here and nights are long and dark.

On winter days, the darkness lasts over 19 hours.

* pronounced 'kara-shock'

North Pole

Karasjok

NORWAY

Arctic Circle

*The **North Pole** is about 2000 kilometres from Karasjok.*

Karasjok is dark in the daytime during the winter

DID YOU KNOW?
The sun does not rise in Karasjok from 21 November to 24 January.

5

Inside the Home

The people of Karasjok are used to dark winters. For them it is a way of life.

Every morning, they put on the lights around their home and leave them on all day.

Some people put candles in their windows or doorways.

The bright light welcomes visitors and passers-by.

DID YOU KNOW?

Most homes in Karasjok have log-burning **stoves.** They give out a warm glow.

6

This house has its lights on all day.

Many people enjoy skiing in the winter.

Going Outside

People don't stay inside all winter. They like to get out into the fresh air.

They have to take care when they go outside. Most people wear **reflectors** so drivers can see them in the dark.

DID YOU KNOW?

People put reflectors on their clothes, shoes, bags and sticks. They even put them on their dogs.

Seeing the Way

People need to be able to see when they are out in the dark. Street lights stay on all the time. The moon shines brightly on clear days. Its light bounces off the white snow. This helps people to see the way.

DID YOU KNOW?
Walkers wear head torches so they can keep their hands inside their mittens.

The snow makes everything look brighter.

11

Keeping Active

People keep active during the winter. They go swimming in the indoor pool or play football in a hall.

There are also lots of sports to do outdoors. People enjoy skiing, **snowboarding** and **sledging**. Children play outside in the dark if it's not too cold.

DID YOU KNOW?

Some ski tracks and slopes have lights so that people can carry on skiing even though it is dark.

The lights on the slopes help people to see where they are going.

Winter Festivals

There are many **festivals** in winter. People celebrate Halloween, Saint Lucia Day and Christmas. Children look forward to the celebrations. There is lots to enjoy in the dark winter.

Everyone enjoys the bright lights of the winter festivals.

15

The Winter Sky

In winter, the sun stays below the horizon. It cannot be seen. But on clear days, it fills the sky with colour. There are deep blues, reds, pinks, lilacs, yellows and greens. It is like a beautiful sunset that lasts all day.

DID YOU KNOW?

In winter, many artists travel to the Arctic to paint the skies.

The days are short but they can be beautiful.

The Northern Lights

Sometimes, coloured lights appear in the sky during the dark winter nights. These lights are called the **Northern Lights**. They can be seen on clear nights from October to March If it is too cloudy, the lights cannot be seen.

DID YOU KNOW?

Many people travel to Norway in winter. They hope to see the Northern Lights.

The Sun Returns

After 60 dark days and nights, the sun returns again. Days grow longer and brighter. People plan snow picnics and **snow scooter** trips. There is still plenty of snow!

DID YOU KNOW?

People eat cakes called sun buns on the day the sun returns.

By the end of January, the sun can be seen once more.

Glossary

arctic part of the Earth to the far north

Arctic Circle line drawn on a map or globe to show the most northern parts of the world

horizon line where the land seems to meet the sky

Northern Lights lights that can be seen in the sky in the winter

North Pole northern-most point on the Earth

reflectors shiny strips that reflect car headlights and help people to be seen

sledging sliding downhill over snow on a sledge

snowboarding standing on a board and sliding over snow

snow scooter vehicle with skis for travelling over snow

stoves metal boxes where you burn wood or coal to heat rooms

twilight soft light in the sky just before it gets dark

Index

A DARK WINTER Claire Llewellyn

Teaching notes written by Sue Bodman and Glen Franklin

Using this book

Developing reading comprehension

This non-chronological report focuses on the town of Karasjok to portray life in the Arctic Circle. The text reports on some of the ways that life is affected by darkness for several months of the year. Key structural non-fiction features to support the reading of information are represented, Maps, captions, labels and 'Did you know?' boxes offer key non-fiction devices.

Grammar and sentence structure

- Sentences follow the language features of the genre style (for example, *'Some people', Most homes', 'People need', 'There are'*).
- Different punctuation styles are used for labels and captions.

Word meaning and spelling

- Adverbial phrases of time (*'On winter days', 'Every morning', 'In winter'*).
- Less familiar vocabulary requiring a glossary to find out its meaning.

Curriculum links

Science – Compare life in the Arctic Circle in the summer months and the winter months. What would be different to the local children's experience? What would be the same? Information could be captured on a Venn diagram.

Art – Using the images of the Northern Lights as inspiration, create Arctic landscapes. First use wax crayons in suitable colours to draw lines and shade in areas for the lights. White crayons can be used to add in stars. Create the night sky by washing over the paper with black or dark blue watercolour paint. The wax resists the paint and creates an aurora borealis effect. Create a snowy foreground by placing a strip of white paper at the bottom and then cutting trees, house and perhaps people, also from white paper.

Learning Outcomes

Children can:

- locate information in the text which supports their comprehension
- use non-fiction features; maps and captions
- problem-solve new topic words that are not completely decodable.

A guided reading lesson

Book Introduction

Give each child a copy of the book. Have them read the title and blurb quietly to themselves.

Orientation

Ask the children what type of text they think this will be. Look together at the title. Ask: *What do you expect to find out about in this book?* Then ask: *What sorts of things might be different, if most of the day was dark?* In addition to the topic of winters with no daylight hours, draw out the purposes of a report and its features, including captions, diagrams, headings, Did you know? boxes.

Preparation

Page 4: Establish that the book focuses on the town of Karasjok (pronounced Ka/ra/shock). Look at the map to see how the town is within the Arctic Circle. Ask the children to look closely at the town's name, possibly using their fingers to frame the word. This word doesn't use the same letter-to-sound relationships as English - it is not pronounced as the letters might suggest- so the children need to become familiar with the word as a whole.

Go back to pages 2 and 3 and ask the children to read the text quietly to themselves. Discuss how photographs show that the autumn and the winter are very different because of the position of the sun. Use the captions to notice how the sun can be seen in the autumn but not the winter.